advances in medicine

Organ Transplants

Henry Wouk

Cavendish
Square
New York

Published in 2014 by Cavendish Square Publishing, LLC
303 Park Avenue South, Suite 1247, New York, NY 10010

Copyright © 2014 by Cavendish Square Publishing, LLC

First Edition

Website: cavendishsq.com

This publication represents the opinions and views of the author based on his or her personal experience, knowledge, and research. The information in this book serves as a general guide only. The author and publisher have used their best efforts in preparing this book and disclaim liability rising directly or indirectly from the use and application of this book.

CPSIA Compliance Information: Batch #WS13CSQ

All websites were available and accurate when this book was sent to press.

Library of Congress Cataloging-in-Publication Data
Wouk, Henry.
Organ transplants / Henry Wouk.
p. cm. – (Advances in medicine)
Includes bibliographical references and index.
Summary: "Discusses the advances that have been made in organ transplantation"–Provided by publisher.
ISBN 978-1-60870-467-5 (hardcover) ISBN 978-1-62712-010-4 (paperback) ISBN 978-1-60870-595-5 (ebook)
1. Transplantation of organs, tissues, etc.–Juvenile literature. I. Title.
RD120.76.W68 2012
617.9'5–dc22
2010042491

Editors: Megan Comerford / Joyce Stanton / Christine Florie
Art Director: Anahid Hamparian   Series Designer: Nancy Sabato

Photo research by Christine Florie and Edward Thomas
Cover photo by *Superstock*: © *Science Faction*

The photographs in this book are used by permission and through the courtesy of:
Cutcaster: ArenaCreative, Back Cover & Openers; AP Images: AOU Careggi hospital, HO, 1, 46; Gene J. Puskar, 24, 36; Michel Springer, 40; Noah Berger, 43. *Alamy*: © Peter Arnold, Inc., 4, 31, 54; © DocCheck Medical Services GmbH, 7, 33; © Olaf Doering, 28; © Arco Images GmbH, 49; *Getty Images*: Dr. David Phillips/Visuals Unlimited, 8; *The Bridgeman Art Library International*: Anatomical diagram, from 'De arte phisicali e de cirurgia' by John Arderne, 1412 (vellum), English School, (15th century) / Royal Library, Stockholm, Swede, 10; Reconstructive surgery on the nose, illustration from 'De curtorum chirurgia per insitionem' by Gaspare Tagliacozzi (1545-99) Venice, published 1597 (engraving) (b/w photo), Italian School, (16th century) / Bibliotheque de la Faculte de Medecine, Paris, France / Archives Charmet, 13; *Superstock*: © Universal Images Group, 14; © Everett Collection, 16; © Blend Images, 26; *Newscom*: Mark Maio, 20; Bob Demay/KRT, 53.

Printed in the United States of America

contents

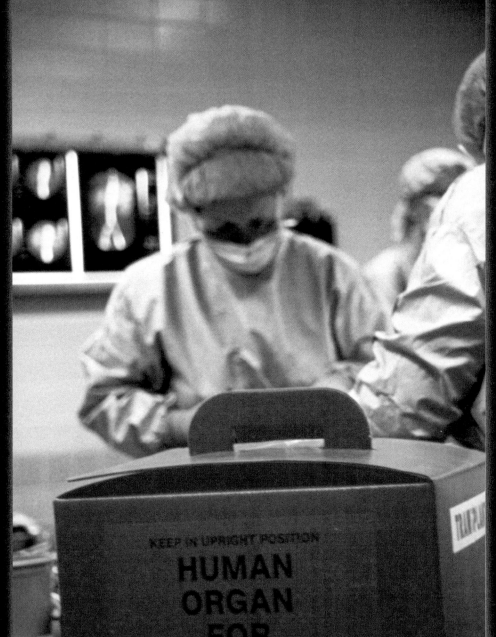

chapter 1

A New Liver for an Olympian

One of the snowboarders who competed in the 2010 Winter Olympics was a young man named Chris Klug. What was amazing about him was not that it was his third Olympics. What was amazing was that he was alive at all. He had been in danger of dying since he was a teenager. The reason was a rare disease that was slowly destroying his liver.

A human organ awaits transplant.

The body needs the liver to make a substance called bile. Bile helps digest food and break it down into substances the body uses to rebuild itself. Klug's bile was not getting from his liver into his digestive system. Doctors gave him various medicines. The drugs would keep him alive and healthy for a while, but they would not cure him.

The only thing that would save Klug was a new liver. If he didn't get one, eventually he would die. For that reason, his doctors planned to perform an organ transplant. This is an operation in which surgeons remove an organ that is defective or worn out and replace it with one that works normally. The healthy organ comes from another person, called an organ donor. Sometimes that donor is a living person. For example, it is possible for one person to give someone else an organ such as a kidney and continue to live a normal life. Most people have two kidneys and can survive with one. But no one can live without a heart or a liver. Those replacements have to come from people who have given permission for their organs to be used after they have died.

The problem is that there are more people who need organs than there are organs available. Klug was put on a special waiting list. He had to wait three years, but one day in 2000, he finally got the phone call he had been hoping for. There was a liver available. It came from a boy who had died in an accident. The boy's family agreed that his organs could be removed and given to anyone who needed them.

The Immune System and Organ Transplants

Taking an organ from one person and putting it in another is a complicated process. The reason is that each person's body has a way of protecting itself from foreign substances that might hurt it. This important protector

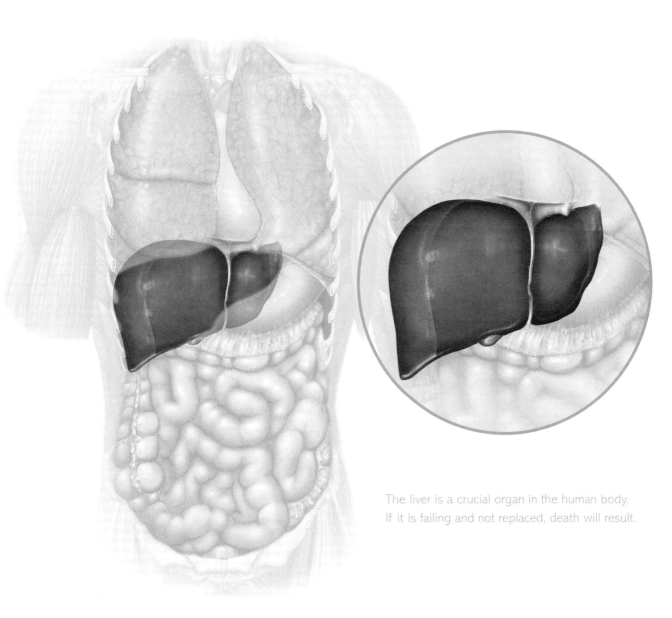

The liver is a crucial organ in the human body.
If it is failing and not replaced, death will result.

is called the **immune system**. The immune system can tell when something that does not belong to the body, such as germs, has invaded it. The immune system keeps the body healthy by attacking the germs, whether they come from a cut on the finger or from contact with a person suffering from a cold.

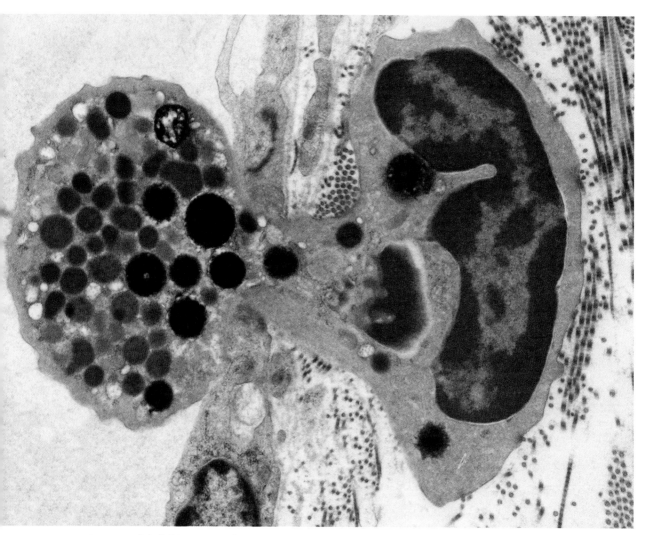

A neutrophil (left), a type of white blood cell, passes through a capillary wall on its way to attack foreign material in the body.

When it comes to organ transplantation, however, this natural means of protection can be a problem. The immune system is geared to react to the new organ the same way it would react to a germ—by attacking it. To prevent this, doctors try to find an organ that is a good match for the patient. That way, the immune system will think the new organ is part of the patient's body. It will be tricked into not ferociously attacking it. Klug was fortunate; his doctors had decided that the boy's liver would be a good match.

Once he got his new liver, Klug also took **immunosuppressant drugs**. These are special drugs that would keep his immune system restrained, like keeping a guard dog on a short leash.

Klug knew he was lucky. If he had been older or a little sicker, doctors might not have been able to save him. In fact, around the time he learned he was getting a new liver, Klug heard that a famous football player, Walter Payton, had just died from the same medical condition he had. Payton was too sick to qualify for a transplant.

After four days in the hospital, Chris Klug went home to recuperate. For the next few weeks he worked on building up his strength. He was determined to compete in the upcoming Winter Olympics. It was hard at first. Taking even a short walk exhausted him. But he kept exercising, kept pushing himself. Four months after his transplant, he was competing in snowboard tournaments. Not long after, he was selected for the 2002 U.S. Olympic Snowboard Team. Klug did so well in that competition that he won a bronze medal, becoming the first athlete with a transplanted organ to win a medal in the Olympics.

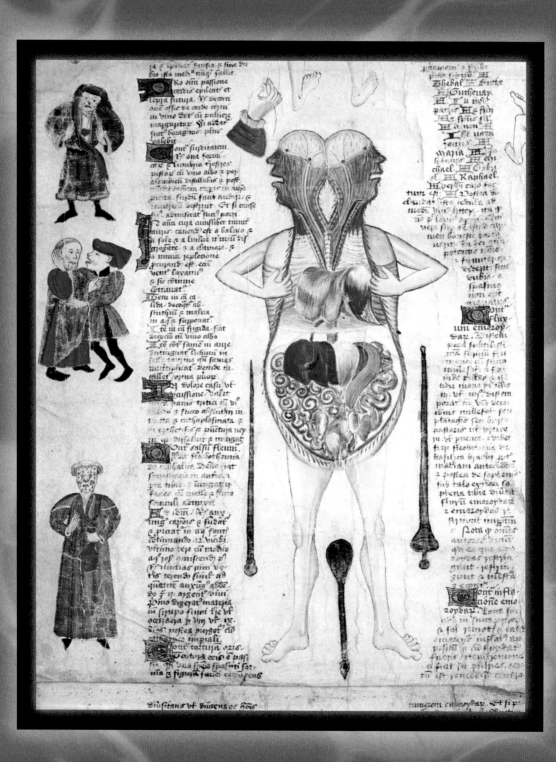

chapter 2

The Early Years

P eople have been getting body parts replaced for centuries. The idea for transplants began when doctors realized they could use pieces of a person's own body to replace missing or defective parts. One of the earliest procedures took place in India during the sixth century BCE. In those days, some criminals were punished by having their noses cut off. A Hindu doctor named Sushruta devised a way to grow skin back, using the patient's own **tissue**, onto the spot where the nose had been. He then reconstructed a new nose using the newly generated skin.

Attempts at medical transplants have been around for centuries.
This anatomical diagram of the human body was created in France in 1412.

It was not until the 1500s that word of this technique made its way to Europe. An Italian doctor named Gaspare Tagliacozzi read about Sushruta's operations and decided to use his procedure to help soldiers who lost their noses in battle. During surgery, Tagliacozzi raised one of the patient's arms to his face and attached a piece of skin from the arm directly to the injured nose. The arm was held in that position with a special kind of sling for about three weeks, until the skin grew onto the nose area. Tagliacozzi then cut away the skin from the arm, leaving the new patch of skin on the face. Then he formed the skin into the shape of a nose.

Another important discovery came a few centuries later, when doctors realized they could take the blood from one person and put it into the body of another who needed it. For many years, no one had even known about **arteries** and **veins**. It was not until 1616 that a British doctor named William Harvey figured out that blood pumps throughout the body through these blood vessels. This discovery gave doctors the idea of connecting some sort of tubing to the blood vessels and injecting liquids into the patient.

At first people thought any kind of liquid would do. Some doctors introduced the blood of calves, lambs, or dogs into their patients. Some even tried milk. Of course, the patients died. It wasn't until two centuries after Harvey's discovery, in 1818, that a British doctor named James Blundell decided that injecting animal blood was too dangerous. He said only human blood was safe to use. He and other doctors began performing **blood transfusions**. They started injecting blood into people who were in danger of bleeding to death.

Not all people did well after blood transfusions. Some got sick and died. This mystified scientists until the early 1900s. That is when Karl Landsteiner,

Gaspare Tagliacozzi used a special method to reconstruct the noses of wounded soldiers.

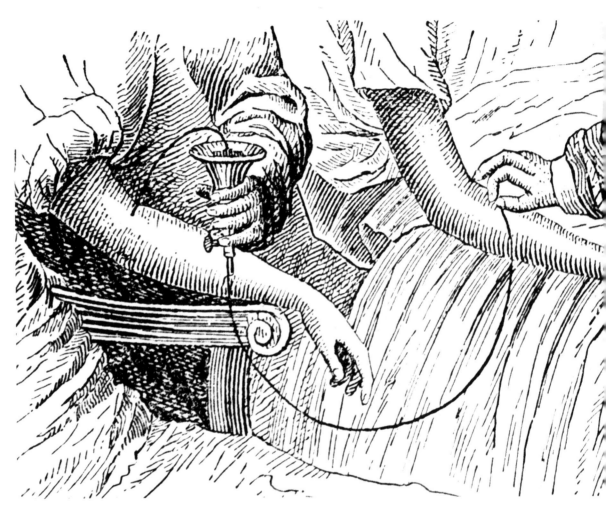

During the late 1800s, blood transfusions were performed in which the donor's blood (left) flowed through tubing, into a cup, and then was pumped into the waiting patient (right).

a doctor from Vienna, Austria, discovered that all human blood was not the same. He and others found that there are four types of blood: A, B, AB, and O. Each person's blood is one of these types. If a patient is given blood that is not compatible with his or her type, he or she can die from the body's reaction to it. Thanks to Landsteiner's discovery, blood from a patient and blood from a donor can be "typed" to make sure that they match, before doctors perform a transfusion.

From 1900 to the 1940s

By the beginning of the twentieth century, there had been several breakthroughs that revolutionized surgery. In 1847 a Hungarian doctor named Ignaz Semmelweis showed that by simply washing their hands before an operation, doctors could eliminate many of the infections that killed their patients. Nearly twenty years later in Scotland, physician Joseph Lister was convincing fellow doctors that using a germ-killing solution to scrub down the operating room and clean the area of the body on which they were about to operate would help more patients survive surgery. In Germany, surgeons noticed that after they sterilized their instruments with steam, patients developed fewer infections. In the United States, an American doctor named Crawford Long made news when he cut a tumor from the neck of a patient. What was amazing was that the man felt no pain. Just before the surgery, Long had soaked a towel in **ether** and had the patient breathe in the fumes. The patient fell into a deep sleep. This discovery of **anesthesia** allowed surgeons to perform complicated operations without inflicting pain, which meant that they could take their time.

The final skills doctors needed to make modern transplant surgery a possibility was introduced by a French doctor named Alexis Carrel. He devised a way to connect tiny blood vessels, which is critical to transplanting

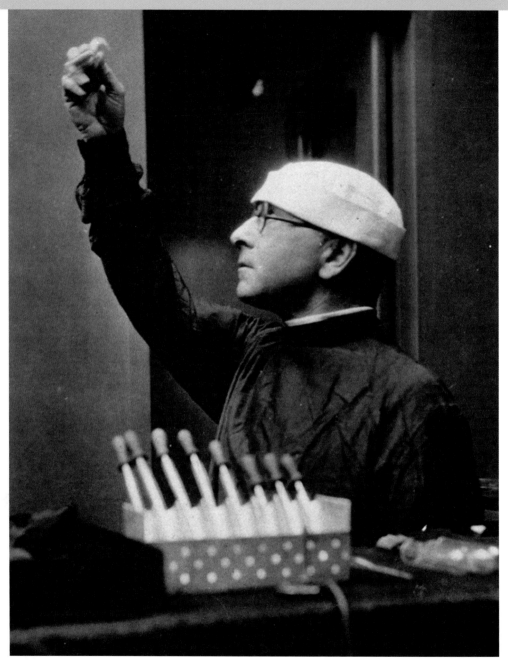

Alexis Carrel won the 1912 Nobel Prize in Physiology or Medicine for his advancements in vascular surgery.

all organs. With cleaner operating rooms, the ability to operate while patients were unconscious, and Carrel's new method of stitching together blood vessels, surgeons at the start of the twentieth century thought they had all they needed to perform transplant operations.

The first successful transplants during this time were with corneas, the clear outer surface of the eye. In 1905 a doctor from Austria named Eduard Zirm helped a blind man see. His patient was a forty-three-year-old farmworker who had accidentally splashed chemicals in his eyes. The chemicals had seared his corneas. The burn scars were so thick that the man could not see anything clearly, though he could detect light.

Zirm had an idea. One of his other patients was an eleven-year-old boy. Something had pierced the boy's right eye. It was so badly damaged that Zirm was going to have to remove it. He asked the boy's father for permission to use part of the cornea to help the blinded farmworker. The father agreed.

Zirm cut out two small, circular sections of the corneas in the farmer's eyes and replaced them with two similar sized circles of tissue from the boy's eye. After the bandages came off, the transplant in the man's right eye became infected. It had to be removed. But the one in the left eye was fine. The man could see well enough to go back to work.

In the early 1900s, corneas were still the only body parts that could be transplanted easily. Researchers eventually discovered that this was because corneas have no blood vessels. As a result, they are invisible to the cells of the body's immune system, which travel through the veins and arteries, searching for invaders.

THE SURGEON AND THE EMBROIDERER

In 1894 people throughout France were horrified when an assassin armed with a knife stabbed their president in the stomach. The razor-sharp blade cut a critical vein. Doctors could do nothing. They had to sit by helplessly as the president bled to death. One person who read about this was a young surgeon from Lyons, France, named Alexis Carrel. He thought that if the president's doctors could have repaired the vein, the president would not have died. Carrel decided to try to find a way to repair damaged blood vessels.

He found the best embroiderer in Lyons and asked her to teach him how to use small needles and fine thread. First, he practiced on sheets of paper, making stitches so small, they were barely visible. Then, he practiced on animals, sewing together the cut ends of blood vessels.

Finally, he was able to apply his skills to humans. This was a hugely important breakthrough. Practically every transplanted organ needs to have blood vessels reattached to it when it is put into the body. Today, doctors still use some of Carrel's techniques and some of the specialized knots he invented.

Carrel moved to the United States in 1904, and he continued to try to improve on surgical techniques. He even worked on an early version of an artificial heart. He was also known for his unusual ideas, such as insisting that the walls and ceilings of his operating room be completely black and that his surgical teams wear black operating gowns. He said the dark color minimized distracting light and let him concentrate better on sewing tiny blood vessels.

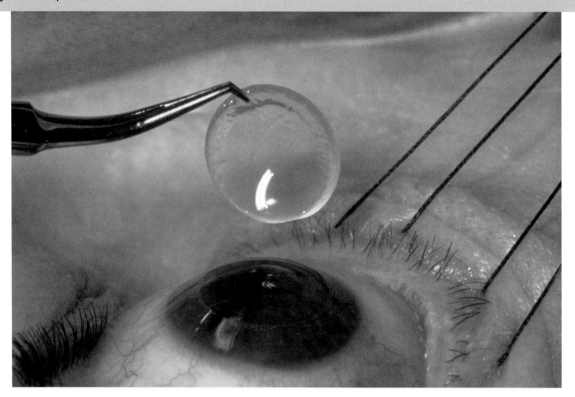

Successful cornea transplants became possible in the early 1900s.

It was not until the 1940s that scientists realized how important the immune system is. The discovery came about when a British biologist named Peter Medawar was trying to help badly burned soldiers during World War II. He noticed that skin transplants from one person to another were not successful and wondered why. After experimenting with skin transplants on animals, he figured out that the body's immune system attacked the skin the same way it would a germ or any other infecting organism.

Once he had learned the reason for the rejection, he wanted to see if there were instances where the immune system did not attack transplanted tissue. In other experiments, he found identical twin cows would not reject skin grafts from each other. Even some nonidentical twin cows would accept transplants from each other. This suggested that the immune system sometimes would accept tissue from another body.

Around this time, doctors decided to try transplanting kidneys. They picked the kidney because it is not complicated to attach. A kidney does not have many blood vessels that need to be connected. Using the techniques developed by Alexis Carrel, doctors could easily attach the few vessels there were. Beginning in the early part of the twentieth century, surgeons all over the world tried kidney transplants. All of the transplants failed. It was not until 1954 that the doctors saw their first success.

The patient was a twenty-three-year-old man named Richard Herrick. Both of his kidneys had failed. This is a dangerous situation, because kidneys filter impurities out of the blood is and expel them in urine. If these substances build up, the body is literally poisoned to death. Herrick would die without a replacement organ. One of the surgeons, Joseph Murray, found out that Herrick had an identical twin brother, Ronald. In desperation, Murray asked Ronald if he would be willing to give his brother one of his kidneys. Ronald said yes.

Richard's life depended on his brother's organ working. The doctors knew that the body often rejected transplanted tissue, but usually not tissue from a twin. If they were wrong, however, Richard Herrick would die. Therefore, they did a series of tests to make sure that the transplant would work, including transferring small patches of skin from one brother to the other. The skin grafts took perfectly, so the doctors went ahead with the kidney transplant surgery.

The operation was a success. Richard's immune system accepted Ronald's kidney, just as Medawar had predicted from his experiments.

After that, the same surgical team did many more kidney transplants between identical twins. All were successful.

However, most people don't have identical twins. Researchers knew that they had to work harder to figure out how to get a person's body to accept a stranger's organ. Some scientists had an idea: since there are different types of human blood, there might also be different types of human tissue. During World War II, French doctor Jean Dausset had noticed that when he gave blood transfusions to some soldiers, they had bad reactions. He began studying blood, particularly the white blood cells that attack germs and transplanted organs. Dausset found a substance on the blood cells that he called HLA, which stands for **human leukocyte antigens**. Every person has different antigens, he discovered, but some people's are more alike than others.

This was a very important discovery. It meant that if a person received an organ from someone with a similar HLA type, his or her immune system would attack the transplant less violently. Gradually, doctors figured out that they could test the tissues of donors and patients. In this way they could find people with similar HLA types. This would help match an organ with a person whose body was more likely to accept it.

Even with close matches, immune systems still attack. Scientists had to figure out a way to hold back the immune system. This is called **immunosuppression**. At first, doctors tried to suppress the immune system with heavy doses of radiation. This did destroy white blood cells, but it also almost killed the patients. Later they tried immunosuppressant drugs that had been used on cancer patients. These helped a little and gave some doctors the courage to try different, more adventurous transplants.

In 1967 Dr. Christiaan Barnard, a surgeon in South Africa, made history when he decided to try what was then the ultimate challenge: a heart transplant. He took the heart of a young woman who had been killed in an accident and put it into a fifty-five-year-old man who was dying of heart failure. The heart started beating almost immediately, and at first the patient did well. However, after eighteen days, his body rejected the new heart, and the man died. Barnard's second transplant, performed a year later, was in a fifty-eight-year-old dentist. This was more of a success. The man lived for about a year and a half.

Within a year, other surgeons were performing heart transplants. However, they were not as skilled with immunosuppression as Barnard, and none of the transplant recipients lived very long. It was years before doctors figured out how to prevent the body from rejecting a new heart yet keep the immune system strong enough to maintain the patient's health.

Late Twentieth Century

The other major organ doctors had been trying to transplant since the early 1960s was the liver. Being able to do that would save many lives. The liver is the largest solid organ in the body and does many important jobs, such as helping the body digest food and filtering waste from the bloodstream. It is a much more difficult organ to transplant than a kidney. A person with a transplanted kidney can be connected to an artificial kidney machine that performs **dialysis** to give the new kidney time to work. There is no backup system for the liver. It has to work immediately after surgery.

For that reason, many surgeons were afraid to try transplanting the liver. But American surgeon Thomas Starzl was fascinated by the challenge.

Transplant pioneer Thomas Starzl oversees a liver transplant in 1989 at the University of Pittsburgh Medical Center.

He set up his own laboratory in an abandoned garage on the grounds of the Miami hospital where he worked. There he studied the liver and experimented with different techniques for removing and replacing it. Starzl eventually developed new ways to match the tissues of a liver donor with a patient. He tried some operations in 1963. When they were not successful, he went back and studied the liver and the immune system to try to figure out where he had gone wrong. Finally, in 1967, he achieved what many thought was impossible—he successfully transplanted a liver into a man dying of liver cancer.

While he was working on liver transplantation, Starzl was also puzzling over how to improve the body's acceptance of other new organs. In the late

1970s he heard of a promising new drug. The drug was called **cyclosporine**. It was extracted from a microscopic fungus found in soil from Wisconsin and Norway. Chemists discovered that cyclosporine blocked specific cells in the immune system that attacked the transplanted organs. When transplant patients took it after surgery, their bodies accepted the new organs more easily. Starzl was so impressed by these results that he almost single-handedly talked the U.S. government into approving cyclosporine for transplants. More and more surgeons began using the drug for all kinds of transplants. Soon the number of successful organ transplants increased, as did the survival rate of patients. In 2008 alone, doctors performed almost 28,000 operations to transplant kidneys and other major organs, such as the pancreas, liver, heart, lung, and intestine. Today, many major organs in the body can be transplanted. The dream that began centuries ago had become a reality.

chapter 3

Transplants Today

By the beginning of the twenty-first century, doctors faced a new set of problems. Once they had figured out how to perform organ transplants, they found it was not easy to find the organs they needed. Things improved in 1984, when the U.S. Congress passed a law that outlawed the sale of human organs and set up a national system to make sure donated organs got to the people who needed them the most.

Finding compatible organs for patients is a crucial step in organ transplants.

Today the process starts when a doctor decides that a transplant is necessary for a patient. The decision is made based on several conditions:

- No other treatment will work. Everything else has been tried or at least considered.
- The patient will die without the transplanted organ.
- The patient is healthy enough to withstand the trauma of the surgery.
- The patient is serious about caring for his or her transplant. Most patients have to take special drugs every day for the rest of their lives and must be prepared to accept this change in lifestyles.

A heart transplant patient prepares her daily medications with the help of her husband.

Once a doctor decides that a patient qualifies for a transplant, the patient is sent to the nearest hospital that has a transplant center. Staff members collect special medical information about the person. They perform blood type and **tissue type tests** so that organ hunters can find the best possible match. The staff also tests for viruses that might damage the transplanted organ. In addition, they do a psychological profile on the patient to make sure he or she will maintain healthy habits and is willing to take daily dosages of the drugs needed to keep the new organ healthy.

Once the transplant center agrees to take on the patient, the medical information is sent to the United Network for Organ Sharing (UNOS), in Richmond, Virginia. UNOS is commissioned by the government to keep a list of every person in the United States who is waiting to receive a kidney, heart, liver, lung, intestine, pancreas, or multiple organs.

On an average day, UNOS links more than a dozen organs with people who need them. The instant an organ becomes available for transplant, a hospital contacts UNOS. Experts there check their records to find everyone who would be a good match for that organ. From that list they pick the best candidate. The person gets the call to go to his or her nearest transplant center immediately. To qualify for an organ, the patient has to be available, still healthy enough to undergo surgery, and ready to have the operation at once.

Many transplanted organs come from someone who has recently died. For that reason, the transplant team has to move quickly. Once an organ is removed from the body of a donor, it is usually flushed with a preservative solution to clear out any remaining blood. Then the organ is packed in ice inside an insulated container, which is carried to a transplant center.

Timing is critical. Hearts and lungs must be used within four to six hours after they have been removed from a body. Kidneys, which can be preserved a little longer, have to be used within one or two days.

How long each transplant candidate spends on the waiting list depends on a variety of things. Age is one factor. Children under twelve years old are usually favored over older patients. The sickest patients typically will get first attention. Even where a person lives makes a difference. Four out of five transplants are performed in the same area of the country where the organs are donated. This is partly because the shorter the distance organs have to travel, the fresher they will be. In bigger states, there are often more people waiting for an organ than in smaller states. Sometimes people will even move to different parts of the country to get on a shorter waiting list.

When Steve Jobs, cofounder and head of Apple, needed a liver transplant in 2008, he was living in California. That year there were more than 1,600 Californians waiting for liver transplants. However, in Tennessee, there were only about 300 people. As a result, he moved to Tennessee to take advantage of the shorter waiting list. He got his liver much sooner than he might have in California.

Medical Miracles

It is hard to overestimate how much transplants have helped people who would have been in great peril a few decades ago. Kidney transplant recipients routinely live longer and longer lives. In 1966 Bill Thompson was a fifteen-year-old boy with failing kidneys. Because of an organ donation from a family friend, he is still healthy more than forty years later. In earlier times a diseased heart would have been a death sentence for Tony Huesman,

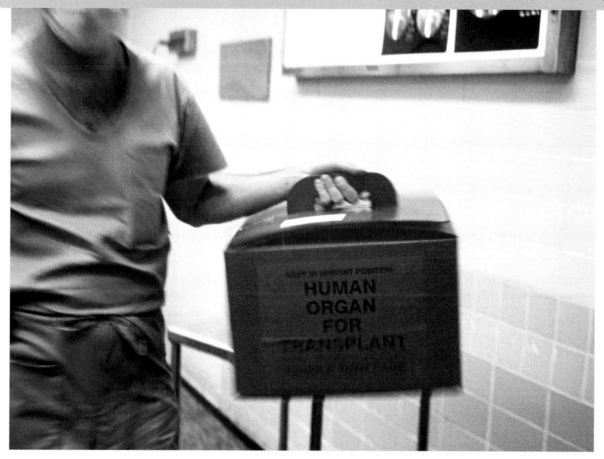

A health-care worker delivers a prepared organ to the operating room.

a teenager who was living in Ohio in 1978. His heart had been weakened by a virus and was quickly losing its ability to pump blood. A heart transplant allowed him to live for thirty-one more years. UNOS has a record of a liver recipient who is still alive more than thirty years after his transplant.

What were considered daring operations only a few decades ago are now everyday events in hospitals all over the country. In 2009 there were more than 16,000 kidney transplants, more than 6,000 liver transplants, and more than 2,000 heart transplants in the United States.

Also becoming more common is something called a multiorgan, or multiple-organ, transplant. In 2008 there were more than eight hundred operations in which the kidney and the pancreas were transplanted together. The pancreas is a small gland that regulates sugar in the blood by secreting substances that help the body use the sugar it absorbs. If it stops working, a person can become diabetic. People who are diabetic sometimes develop kidney failure and need kidney transplants. By giving a person a new pancreas as well as a new kidney, doctors remove the threat of diabetes and protect the new kidney.

Doctors have also begun to transplant the heart and lungs together. Small children with heart defects often have defective lungs as well. Surgeons have found that sometimes the simplest way to fix this condition is to replace both organs. Today, transplanting several organs at once is so common that many hospitals now have doctors who are multiorgan transplant specialists.

The Frankenstein Factor

The story of a scientist who puts together a new creature—Frankenstein—from the limbs and body parts of several people has long been popular. It is still fiction, but maybe not for long. As surgeons have gotten more skilled at transplanting organs, they have moved on to transplanting other parts of the body. For example, since the 1970s doctors have been able to reattach fingers or even hands that had been cut off in accidents. Once they had mastered the surgical skills to do that, it was only a matter of time before someone wanted to transplant a limb from one person to another.

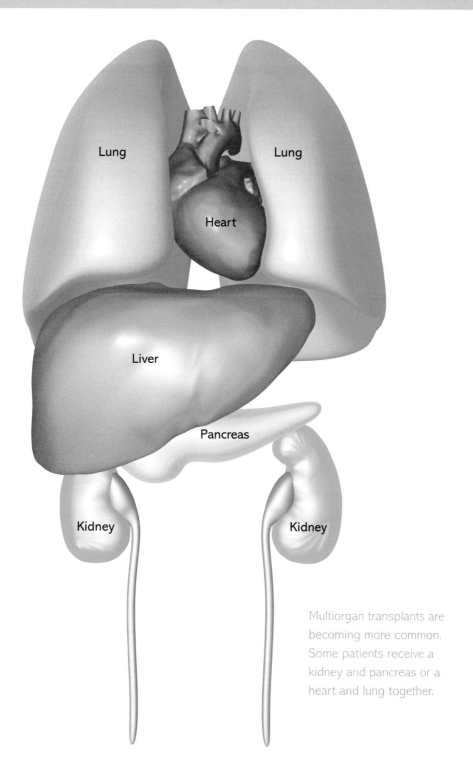

Lung

Lung

Heart

Liver

Pancreas

Kidney

Kidney

Multiorgan transplants are becoming more common. Some patients receive a kidney and pancreas or a heart and lung together.

THE GIRL WITH FIVE NEW ORGANS

What began as persistent stomachaches for Brooklyn teenager Kristin Molini turned out to be a deadly problem with her entire digestive system. By the time she was a sophomore in high school, she had to have part of her intestine removed to reduce the pain. A few months later, the pain came back, and she needed more surgery. At times she had to be fed through a special tube inserted into her abdomen, bypassing her stomach. After she graduated high school, she had to undergo a third operation, then a fourth. Nothing seemed to help for very long.

It turned out that she had a rare medical condition in which her stomach muscles and the muscles in her digestive tract were paralyzed. She could not eat and digest food properly. By 2006 her condition had become so bad that doctors told her she would need a new stomach, pancreas, and small intestine. A year later, while she was waiting for these organs, her liver failed. Then she needed four organs. In 2009 her large intestine began to fail. She needed five organs. Her weight dropped to 74 pounds (33.6 kilograms).

In 2009 New York-Presbyterian Hospital/Columbia University Medical Center in New York City called with news. They had located matching organs from a boy in Mississippi who had died in an accident. Doctors removed all five organs and replaced them during a thirteen-hour operation. Before the surgery, Molini had been so weak that she spent most of her days lying on the couch at home. A few months after, she was celebrating New Year's Eve by going out dancing with friends.

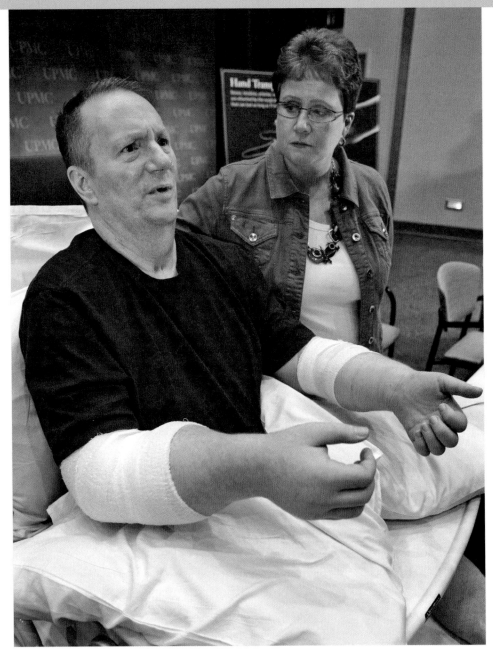

This man received a double hand transplant. The surgery took nine hours.

In 2008 German surgeons performed the world's first double-arm transplant on a farmer named Karl Merk. He had lost both of his arms in a machinery accident six years earlier and had little more than stumps below his shoulders. It took a forty-person surgical team more than fifteen hours to transplant the two arms, but the operation was a huge success. A year after the surgery, the fifty-four-year-old man was able to lift his arms, ride a bicycle, eat without help, and hug his children. His future plans are to go back to work on his farm and start riding his motorcycle again.

Even more dramatic than limb transplants are face transplants. Once a fantasy, these are now a medical reality. Surgeons have been able to take one person's face and surgically attach it it onto someone else's head. The first operation of this sort was done in 2005. French surgeons in the city of Lyons agreed to help a thirty-eight-year-old woman named Isabelle Dinoire, whose face had been horribly mauled by her dog. Her mouth, chin, and part of her nose and cheeks had been ripped away. Doctors had told her that a series of plastic surgeries over three years could fix some, but not all, of the damage. She didn't want to do it. Then they proposed what no one had done before: a single surgery in which they would perform a partial-face transplant. They would remove the lower part of the face from a recently deceased woman and place it over the damaged areas on Dinoire's face. They predicted that her body would gradually accept the transplant. The result would not be her face or the donor woman's face, but something in between—an entirely new, usable face.

The surgery took more than half a day. It required attaching blood vessels and nerves so small that surgeons had to use a microscope to see them.

HANDY TRANSPLANT

One of the most famous hand-transplant operations happened in 1998. That year a team of Australian surgeons had perfected what they thought was the best surgical method for transplanting a hand from a donor to a recipient. They needed to test the technique. They found an ex-convict from New Zealand named Clint Hallam. Fourteen years earlier, he had lost his right hand in an industrial accident in prison. He was willing to be the test patient for the operation.

The next challenge for the surgeons was to find a hand. There was nothing available in Australia, but they heard that there was a hand in France. A young man had died in a motorcycle accident, and tests showed that his tissue was a close match to Hallam's.

The surgeons and Hallam flew to Lyons, France. There a team of Australian and French surgeons spent fourteen hours carefully attaching the nerves, tendons, arteries, and veins from the dead man's hand to Hallam's forearm. Everything went well. Hallam's new hand could feel heat, cold, and pain. After a while, he could hold his cell phone with his new right hand, manage a knife and fork, hold a glass of water, and even write with it.

Doctors in other parts of the world were so encouraged by the results that they tried their own operations. By 2001, nine other people had received new hands. Three of them underwent double-hand transplants. Those patients were doing well, but Clint Hallam was not. His hand looked red and infected. He admitted to his doctors that he did not always take his medication to control the body's immune rejection, as he was supposed to. Hallam also began to complain that the hand looked ugly. It did not resemble his left hand. He said he felt "detached" from it.

Finally, in 2001, a little more than two years after having the surgery, Hallam said he wanted the transplanted hand removed. The doctors reluctantly agreed. They flew him to London where, during a secret operation, the same doctors who had performed the world's first successful hand transplant removed the hand. They fitted him for a prosthetic, or artificial, hand. In spite of Hallam's experience, hand transplants have become more common. By 2009 more than thirty had been performed all over the world.

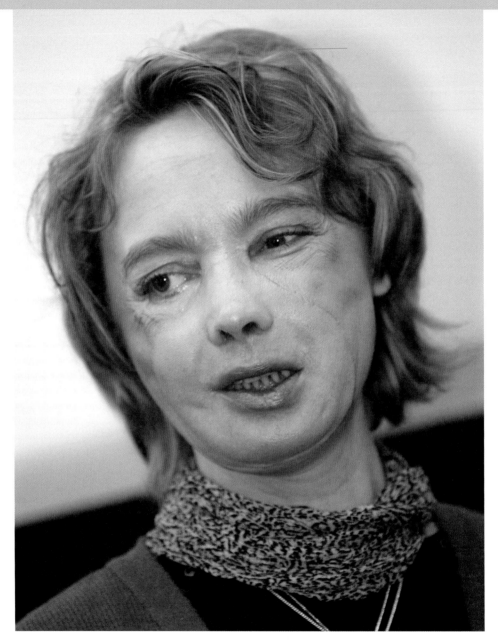

In 2005 Isabelle Dinoire received a new nose, chin, and mouth in a groundbreaking transplant operation in France. This photo was taken one year after her surgery.

Twenty different muscles had to be connected from Dinoire's face to the nose, mouth, and cheeks of the dead woman's face.

After it was all over, doctors were concerned that the new face might be rejected or that it would be simply a mask of skin. Neither problem happened. Within a year and a half, Dinoire had nearly complete control of her new face. Five years after the surgery, she is healthy and can smile.

Since Dinoire's surgery, at least ten face transplants have been done around the world. All those done before 2010 were partial, like Dinoire's. It was not until the spring of 2010 that the first full-face transplant was performed. It was done in a hospital in Barcelona, Spain. The patient was a young man who had barely survived a shotgun blast to the face. After he learned about Isabelle Dinoire's surgery, he asked doctors in Barcelona to help him.

An international team of thirty surgical specialists removed the entire face of the donor. This included all the skin, muscles, and lips, as well as the teeth, cheekbones, and jawbone. They placed the donor face on the injured man's skull. The reattachment was so elaborate, it took the team an entire day. The man survived.

The world's second full-face transplant was performed two months later, by surgeons in France. Today there seems to be no limit to what can be transplanted.

The Great Organ Shortage and Other Problems

Despite all these amazing successes, there are troubling moral issues surrounding the field of transplant medicine. One is deciding who should get the organs. Today a patient's place on a waiting list depends on the urgency of his or her medical condition. But what about someone who has been a heavy smoker all of his or her life and now needs new lungs? Should that person be put ahead of another lung-transplant candidate who has never smoked? Or what about someone whose excessive use of alcohol has damaged his or her liver? Should that person get a new liver before someone who is not a drinker?

At the moment, a transplant candidate's unhealthy habits are not considered in deciding who gets a transplant, but some people think they should be. People still talk about the famous Irish soccer player George Best, who received a new liver in 2002. He was known to have been an alcoholic. Many people were outraged when, after the transplant surgery, he was seen drinking. He died three years later of multiple-organ failure, in part because of his heavy drinking. Some felt he should not have been given a new liver that could have saved someone else's life.

Another problem concerns how transplant medicine has moved on from life-or-death operations to transplanting limbs and faces. Some doctors and transplant experts wonder if this is frivolous, because there are still many people whose lives depend on getting critical organs. They say that surgeons should be using their skills to help save those lives instead of spending time on expensive and time-consuming cases that are not a matter of life or death.

However, the biggest challenge the medical field faces today is what to do about the shortage of organs. There are more people who need organs than there are organs available. In the United States, the number of people who need transplants has grown steadily. In October 2008 it topped 100,000 for the first time, and it has stayed at that level ever since. At the same time, the number of organs being donated has been decreasing. As a result, more people on waiting lists die before they get a transplant. For example, in 2007 there were more than 80,000 people on the waiting list for kidneys, but only

Today, there is a great demand for organs. Unfortunately, there are more people in need of new organs than there are donors.

about 16,000 people got new kidneys. That same year nearly 5,000 people on the waiting list died. (In 2013, 96,000 people were on the waiting list for new kidneys.)

"Transplant tourism" is one result of this organ shortage. According to Nancy Scheper-Hughes, a professor of medical anthropology at the University of California, Berkeley, wealthy people from Europe and the United States who need kidney transplants but don't want to wait have been buying the organs from poor people in other parts of the world. The wealthy "tourist" who needs a kidney may fly to another country and have the transplant surgery done there. Or the tourist may pay for the donor to come to his or her country. Either way, the donors are paid a great deal of money for their kidneys. One man from Spain traveled to China and paid $180,000 to have a kidney transplant.

Scheper-Hughes located a website in China that offered to sell pieces of livers from still-living people. This business goes on everywhere, even in the United States. In 2009 a Brooklyn man was arrested for selling human organs. He had promised an undercover FBI agent that he would find him a kidney from a live human being for $160,000. To stop this, many countries have laws outlawing the sale of human organs.

Some countries, such as Iran and Singapore, go even further. The governments there will pay their citizens if they donate a kidney or other body part for transplant. Those countries appear to have less of a problem with kidney shortages than the United States does.

Today in the United States, people can check a box on their driver's license to indicate that they want to be organ donors. However, European countries such as France, Spain, and Austria have a different system. They require people to say they do not want to be donors. If people do not specifically say so, their organs can be taken when they die. The system seems to work, since these countries have fewer organ shortages. Today, lawmakers in Illinois, New York, Pennsylvania, and Texas have suggested copying this system, but so far no new laws have been passed.

chapter 4

The Future of Transplants

If more than a half century of medicine has proven anything, it's that when something in the human body breaks down, it is often possible to replace it. Already surgeons have been able to transplant organs that they once considered unusable. It had been thought that there was an age limit on donated organs. But doctors in Canada disproved this by using the liver of a ninety-two-year-old woman to extend the

A surgical team transplants a windpipe into a cancer patient with a procedure that uses stem cells to regenerate tissue.

life of a much younger woman. There was a time when kidney patients who received their organs from cadavers, or dead bodies, needed several transplants over their lifetimes. The reason was that kidneys from cadavers did not last as long as those from living donors. Today, new antirejection drugs keep cadaver kidneys working longer, freeing up organs for other people.

Then there is the question of where to get organs. Today, doctors get most material for transplants from two sources. For a skin graft they often use skin from another part of the patient's own body. This kind of transplant is called an **autograft**. Organs or tissues that are transplanted from one person, living or dead, to another are called **allografts**. (*Allo* comes from a Greek word that means "other.")

But there is a third type of transplant called a **xenograft**. (*Xeno* comes from the Greek word for "stranger.") This type of transplant is the grafting of tissue from an animal to a human. Xenografts are nothing new. For decades, surgeons have been fixing defective human hearts with valves taken from the hearts of pigs and cows. For a long time, too, doctors have dreamed of doing more complicated operations–transplants of entire organs taken from animals. Some of these operations were tried in the 1980s and 1990s, but with little success.

Part of the problem in using animal organs is getting the human body to accept them. Another is the risk that the organs might infect people with nonhuman diseases that the human immune system cannot control. However, some researchers still think that animal-to-human transplants may someday be possible, and that the animal that may make this happen is the pig. Research scientists have been studying pigs for years because their organs are about the same size as those of humans, and because pigs don't seem to have any diseases that can infect people. Researchers in Great Britain and in the United States have already found the **genes** that cause the human immune system to reject pig tissue. Scientists at the University of Missouri have used **genetic engineering** to **clone**, or make copies of, pigs without these genes. No transplants have been tried yet, but in the future there may be organ farms where animals are bred for providing organs for people.

Researchers have been studying the possibility of animal to human transplants. Pig organs are roughly the same size as human organs and seem to pose no risk of disease transmission.

THE HEART OF A BABOON

In October 1984, Stephanie Fae Beauclair was born at Loma Linda University Medical Center in California. Doctors had sad news for her parents. The newborn girl's heart was defective—too defective to fix. She would soon die.

There was one thing that might possibly save her: a heart transplant. It would be an unusual heart transplant, however. It would not be a human heart the little girl would receive but one from a seven-month-old baboon that had been raised in the medical center for research purposes. Doctors selected a baboon because these animals are not an endangered species and because their organs are very similar to those of humans.

Doctors said that with the right amount of immunosuppressant drugs, the transplant might work. It was the only hope. The infant's parents agreed to try it. After the operation, the doctors were pleased

50

to see the animal heart beat normally. The baby looked healthy. The hospital announced to the world that the infant, known then only as Baby Fae, had made medical history. She was the first infant to have an animal-heart transplant.

Sadly, after two weeks, Baby Fae's body rejected the heart, and she got sick. She died three weeks after the surgery.

A few years later, in 1992, surgeons tried another baboon organ transplant at a hospital in Pittsburgh, Pennsylvania. This time the patient was a thirty-five-year-old man. He had a disease called hepatitis B, which was destroying his liver and would eventually kill him. The doctors knew that hepatitis B attacks human livers but not the livers of baboons. The man agreed to try the transplant. Unfortunately, an undetected virus in the new liver attacked his body. He lived for only seventy-one days.

Mechanical Parts?

Other scientists have been working on ways to replace organs the way we now replace parts in a car—they've been making artificial body parts. Ever since the 1950s, scientists have worked to build a human-made heart. Robert Jarvik designed the first artificial heart that worked well. It was implanted in a retired Seattle dentist, Barney Clark, in 1982. Clark knew the risks, but his own heart was so fragile that he volunteered to be a test subject. Doctors at the University of Utah implanted the aluminum and plastic heart in Clark and hooked it up to pumping machinery the size of a small refrigerator. Clark lived for a little less than four months.

Today there is an improved model, also invented by Jarvik, called the Jarvik 2000. This artificial heart is meant to be temporary. It keeps the patient alive until a real heart becomes available for transplant. The AbioCor, a battery-powered pump about the size of an adult's fist, also helps keep patients alive temporarily. Both of these devices have to be connected to a large power unit.

A major technological breakthrough took place in May 2010, when forty-three-year-old Charles Okeke got a new kind of artificial heart. Okeke received a more compact, portable device called the SynCardia heart. For the first time in the history of human-made organs, the patient was able to leave the hospital. When it was time to go home, Okeke strapped on a 13-pound (5.9 kg) backpack with a miniaturized pumping unit and left the hospital. The SynCardia heart was meant to buy him time while he waited for a real heart to become available, but he was not confined to a hospital bed while he waited.

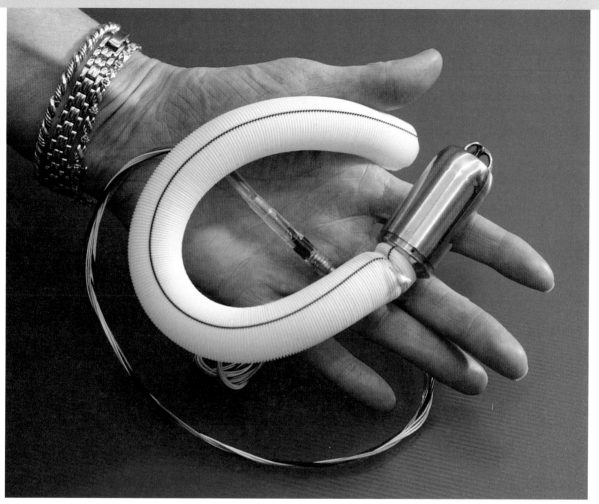

The Jarvik 2000 is an artificial heart meant to be used on a temporary basis.

Researchers have been trying to build other artificial organs as well. In California and Ohio, scientists have devised something called a wearable kidney. It is a 10-pound (4.5-kg) unit the user wears outside the body, like a large fanny pack. Someday doctors hope to shrink it down to about the size of a cell phone and implant it just under the skin.

The Secret of Stem Cells

The ultimate organ replacements might come from patients themselves. Scientists hope to create new organs using a patient's own tissues. The secret is **stem cells**. These are basic cells from which specialized body cells develop. Researchers have been learning ways to manipulate them so that the stem cells grow into specific types of cells, such as liver cells for a patient who needs a new liver.

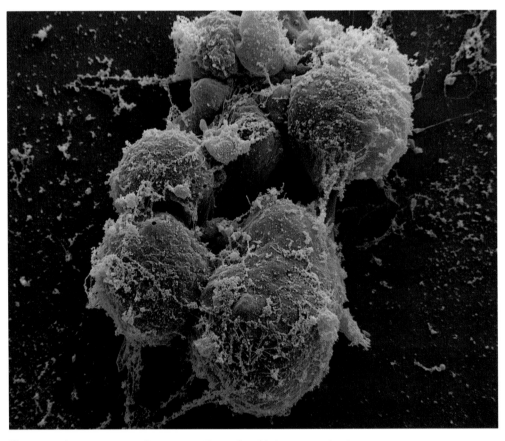

These are human stem cells as seen through a high-powered microscope.

In 2008 doctors in Spain used stem cells to treat a female patient who needed a new trachea, or windpipe. Her trachea had been damaged by tuberculosis. Doctors first took a trachea from another person and then stripped it of all the cells that belonged to the donor. What was left was the protein "skeleton" of the trachea. They then took stem cells from the patient's bone marrow, which is the place where some of these cells are formed. They processed them to become skin cells and cartilage cells. The doctors then immersed the trachea skeleton in the specialized cells. Gradually the specialized cells covered the skeleton. The result was something that was perfectly compatible with the patient's body. Since it was a perfect match, the woman did not need to take immunosuppressant drugs. The surgery was such a success that doctors now look forward to the time when they can grow more complicated organs. When that day comes, there will be no more waiting lists, no more organ shortages, no more transplant tourism. We will each be our own best organ donor.

Glossary

allografts Tissues or organs that are transplanted from one human to another.

anesthesia Drugs introduced prior to surgery that inhibit the sense of pain.

arteries Blood vessels that carry blood from the heart to the rest of the body.

autograft Any tissue that is taken from one place on a person's body and grafted to another place on the same person's body.

blood transfusion Transfer of blood into a person's body.

clone To make an identical biological copy of something.

cyclosporine A drug taken after an organ transplant to keep the recipient's body from rejecting the new organ.

dialysis A medical procedure that does the job of a kidney by filtering out waste products from the blood.

ether A medical inhalant anesthetic.

gene The pattern of chemicals in a cell that carries information about the qualities of a living thing from its parents.

genetic engineering The technology of changing the genetic structure of an organism.

human leukocyte antigens Molecules, or markers, on the surface of a cell that the immune system uses to identify the body's own cells.

immune system The body's system of self-protection against diseases and the germs that cause them.

immunosuppressant drugs Drugs that inhibit or weaken the immune system.

immunosuppression An action that weakens the immune system's response to foreign substances.

stem cells The general body cells that can become specialized cells.

tissue A part of an organism made up of a large number of cells that have similar structure and function.

tissue type tests A series of tests done to see if the tissue or organ of a donor is compatible with the body of the person who will receive it.

veins Blood vessels that carry blood to the heart from the rest of the body.

xenograft The grafting of tissue from one species, such as a pig or cow, to another, such as a human.

Find Out More

Books

Campbell, Andrew. *Organ Transplants*. Mankato, MN: Smart Apple Media, 2010.

Farndon, John. *From Laughing Gas to Face Transplants*. Chicago: Heinemann, 2008.

Grey, Susan Heinrichs. *Transplants*. Ann Arbor, MI: Cherry Lake Publishing, 2009.

Websites

Center for Organ Recovery & Education (CORE)
www.core.org/default.asp
The Center for Organ Recovery & Education is a Pennsylvania-based organization that actively seeks donors for those needing transplants.

Organ Transplantation—Medline Plus: U.S. National Library of Medicine and the National Institutes of Health
www.nlm.nih.gov/medlineplus/organtransplantation.html
A U.S. government review of anything and everything involving organ transplants.

Scientific Registry of Transplant Recipients
www.srtr.org
The Scientific Registry of Transplant Recipients is a database of transplant statistics.

University of Rochester Medical Center
www.urmc.rochester.edu/encyclopedia/content.cfm?pageid=P03066
The University of Rochester Medical Center online encyclopedia has an excellent description of the history of organ transplantation and social issues surrounding it.

U.S. Government Information on Organ and Tissue Donation and Transplantation
www.organdonor.gov
A valuable site that provides the latest U.S. statistics on organ transplants and information on how to become a donor.

World Health Organization: Human Transplantation
www.who.int/transplantation/en/
The shortage of organs for transplants is a worldwide problem that the World Health Organization describes on this site.

Index

Page numbers in **boldface** are illustrations.

About the Author

Henry Wouk has authored more than a dozen books on health and science, and has written for a wide variety of national magazines. He lives in Massachusetts.